MARGINAL ROAD

ALSO BY RACHEL M. SIMON

Theory of Orange

Marginal Road

A Chapbook

Rachel M. Simon

Hollyridge Press
Venice, California

© 2009 RACHEL M. SIMON

All rights reserved under International and Pan-American Copyright Conventions. Published in the United States by Hollyridge Press.

Hollyridge Press
P.O. Box 2872
Venice, California 90294
www.hollyridgepress.com

Cover and Book Design by Rio Smyth
Cover Image by © Mariya Kondratyeva | Dreamstime.com
Author photo by Karen Schechner
Manufactured in the United States of America by Lightning Source

ISBN-13: 978-0-9799588-7-8
ISBN-10: 0-9799588-7-3

Grateful acknowledgment is made to the editors of the following publications where these poems first appeared:

H_NGM_N: "Good Government" and "Soul Within Woman"
The Insider: "Disability of Grief"
The Westchester Review: "Game One of the World Series With Your Father" and "Nixzmary"

"A Story About My Body" borrows its title from Robert Haas
"Lift Off" borrows its couch and astronauts from Dean Young
"Nixzmary" also appears in *Theory of Orange* (courtesy of Pavement Saw Press)

16 15 14 13 12 11 10 09   10 9 8 7 6 5 4 3 2 1

Contents

Good Government	3
Game One of the World Series with Your Father	4
My Family of Eaters	5
Late November	7
Soup Thermos	8
The Ketchup Bottle	9
Postmark from the Transition	10
Seizure	11
Your Mother Pregnant With You	12
P.A.R.A.	13
A Story About My Body	14
Homecoming	15
The Civil Evangelical	16
Ten Thousand Hours	17
Lift Off	18
America's Next Top Poet	19
Pillow Sonata	20
You are Mist	21
In the Aftermath	23
The Soul Within Woman	24
A Mixture of Frailties	25
The Man Behind Me on the Train	26
Nixzmary	27
De Compose	28
Disability of Grief	29
After Life	30
On The Occasion of Edna Parker's Death	31
Juvenescence	32
Boys Who Need Haircuts	33
Adolescence is No Joke	34
Alphabet Acrostic	35
Another Acrostic	36

Marginal Road

GOOD GOVERNMENT

After 27 years of adequate hearing aids and a shake of lip-reading,
Ohio bought state-of-the-art aids for Sweets and she hears
her first banana peel. The noisy revelation emptied her crisper,
which sounded plastic, more funky. To open produce aloud, unsung.

In noisy lives of history and eucalyptus we never think banana peel.
Cinematic tomato squish, quiet cat feet outside the house,
muffled background crashes on the Fisher Price recording of you
singing flat notes to the chronologically appropriate pop song.

I'm trying to capture the skitter and thrum
to package for the trip to Cleveland,
learning dog signs for Definitely,
to avoid the love-maul for our language barrier.

The degradable city freezes and thaws,
thankful to have its homers,
the occasional small point spread,
Marginal Road, thick skin of security.

When Sweets throws a silent party in the listening gallery
wear thick socks on deep shag carpet,
whiff the hors d'oeuvres, don't chew.

GAME ONE OF THE WORLD SERIES WITH YOUR FATHER

The rooting is genetic: learn disappointment.
Next year, next year, now?
The ticket lottery sibling competitive.
Daily phone calls of strategy unheard by pitching staff.

A reasonably priced flight,
once in fifty-nine years,
an inconvenient airport,
project, donkey, Jhonny with an h.
Choose a player: facial hair makeover,
one for grand slams.
The racial insensitivity of scalpers
and Wahoo cut by mid-memorabilia.

We are marrow charged.
Fully outfitted for the day.
The testosterone thick
for levitation and towel swinging.
A better spitter, two-seam curve, breaking ball.

Raucous forty-four thousand, on our feet, together.
Build your memory directory with this.

MY FAMILY OF EATERS

eulogized Zadie
with slurping noises.
We remember the eating.

My grandmother ate deliberately,
aware of every bite at the table
in her pink silver wallpaper kitchen.
Meals ended with assessment:
the size of your helpings
and correction with wrist and spoon.

My mother's impressed by your
revolutionary salad
balanced bites of crisp and crunch
a delight among women
a potluck revelation.

My father's favorites are sweetened
with the highest of fructose
and colored red #5
and even then enhanced
with a love dusting of powdered sugar.

My brother's youth was spent
with the fingers of chickens,
hot dogs bunless and plain.
An adult he's developed a relationship
with a famous sausageier,
blends goat cheese and boar meat
on Chicago's north side.

My palate is raw
ripe cheeses

and clarified butters
a tasting menu tour of small plates
and cheap eats
the courses quiet revelation,
taste buds attuned.

I married the food focused
near vegetarian meat aficionado
supporting community agriculture
a tireless ingredient reader

Out to dinner we diverse,
we seafood and breads,
we focus on the plate's shape
the oblong. Inconsistently aware of charm
and elbow placement.

LATE NOVEMBER

Every lunch sack contains a turkey sandwich
the Monday after Thanksgiving.
United: poultry, potatoey, we trudge back
to desks and jackhammers. Parts of our day
resemble standardized tests. Everybody's neck
loses a bit of head-holding strength.
The city slid halfway down the hill.
The cost of seeing your childhood roof,
the place you learned to inhale a cigarette,
from a decommissioned spy satellite
now dedicated to time consuming
nostalgia fluffing on the company dime.

SOUP THERMOS

hot soup promise
office afternoon
tomato based or chicken stock
socks and spoon
lid as bowl, steam suspended
to coat esophageal membrane
no comfort in cold
every igloo uncozy
this thermos a direct
Kermit reference
each spoonful
the doorknob turning
wooden bench worn smooth
three generations
seasoning the cast iron
well-timed invitation

THE KETCHUP BOTTLE

left by our third date's drive-in waitress
on our third date, discarded by my mother
afraid of red poisons on her doorstep.
Replacement bottle pinched on purpose
sent in a box labeled rye whiskey
dangerous a dry 1962 OU dorm.
Hidden behind wool skirt's
maturing guffaw.

In mundane American car outside
Boulevard Elementary where
"We've been dating a while."
signals breakup, disoriented,
when the shaky ketchup bottle
appears, wearing an engagement ring.

The bottle contained
red, vinegar, sweet.
Transformed tomato product
not canvas but symbol.
Sure it's red, but not humorless.

POSTMARK FROM THE TRANSITION

1. the name altered from parent's choosing
2. the threshold of a home
3. white gloves on the windowsill
4. costumes of our drama
5. soup stock of animal and stone
6. thigh, syringe
7. non-ninety degree staircase
8. redistribution of fats
9. your mother's voice in the next room
10. orphaned pair of pants
11. disappearing ink dots
12. recollections of family hot fudge
13. rigid posture attempts
14. dude descending a staircase
15. handclasp, handshake, embrace

SEIZURE

Julius Caesar's haircut was suburban popular
in 1992. Specifically at Marsh Lane and
Trinity Mills Road where you can play
out-of-date video games for a nickel
and get your tires rotated. Caesar's tires
were wooden, which is why his salad—
festooned with anchovies and parmesan—
has the highest self-esteem in a wooden bowl.
The hair is a Caesar not a bowl cut.
It will disguise the first three centimeters
of a receding hairline. Nobody will criticize
your hair when you have a seizure.
They'll likely remember that you peed
on the floor, or how your bit tongue bled.
The seizure is named for Caesar, a famous
epileptic who snatched the naming rights from
Lenin and Napoleon. Gonorrhea
could have been named Napoleon
which would make little difference
in how badly coaches teach sex education.
Their legacy embodied when test results
confirm burning infection, the aftertaste of Caesar
wrapped in his laurels, steady on top of his head
cushioned as he slumps toward the ground.

YOUR MOTHER PREGNANT WITH YOU

cravings unremarkable, sleep unrestful
imagines you gruesome, talented,
she considers risks, thinks of hair,
considers organs and piano lessons,
scowls at her bladder compression,
lists of names, gender consideration,
your mother vetoed every name
from her seventh grade,
they are not custodial arts
the way your mother practices them,
biology and heredity, braces,
worst traits worst relatives,
feels pregnant in her bent knees,
considers pain, broken anatomy
enumerated, recollection pain relief,
her vomit was green, twins, hemorrhoids,
today you and your mother are not pregnant

P.A.R.A.
People Against Rachel and Andy
Bent Tree West, Texas, 1990

I expect the founders have forgotten
the club identified only by its initials
conceived by tweens
before the term was coined
to ostracize me from my middle rung
of sixth grade popularity.

The club expanded by an A
when the school bus
hand holding was discovered
before we knew it was ok to let go
to avoid handling after school
snacks with pruned fingers.

We remember our tormentors by name.
Inexpertly psychoanalyzing
Susan Schultz and Scott Berlin.
The German front closing in
from one block away
in every direction of a subdivision
named for the bend in a tree.

Eighteen years after pubescent shame
Susan Schultz shows up in every
high school workshop I teach
to alarm the actual fourteen-year-olds
with my mold-filled wound.

In questioning their motivations
are they declared the winners?
In honoring their organization
expert jealousy.

A STORY ABOUT MY BODY

When I broke my pancreas
I tried a flood of huge
caffeine-free plastic cups.
When that didn't work
I hid cupcakes in a drawer
without syringes to build courage,
my leg: puncturable anatomy.
I lost an inch of intended height:
puberty promised five seven
collided with Arsenio and virus.
My first wrinkle is at eye level
with my should-have-been
asymmetrical nose.
Expected punishments
internal freckles
and their cashmere sisters.

HOMECOMING

Texas folksingers are always inviting me
on their porch, sweet tea still air.

I'm from a place you expect
friendly to your face.

Local commodities: excruciating aesthetics,
dooley pick ups, and flat.

Export compassionate. Generations
close to the Alamo expect defeat.

THE CIVIL EVANGELICAL

reminds me to floss more often,
investigate what might be fungus
under a nail. He is the bruise
wakes you up itching.

The union of theological certainty
and Hawaiian shirt rankles punch lines
and powers higher. But the shirt volume
distracts from internal revolt personified
in skin sores distant from the palm.

Stained glass stains are easily removed
by mixing healthy self with comfortable
women's shoes. It isn't dogmatic
when you rip methodically, razor remove
offending passages.

Their songs stuck in your head years later
in time zones uncondoned, bricks
manufactured ovenless. The work
of gathering seeds in your hands.
Comfortable space alongside ideas.

Your tour guide and mine
separate shoulder pads.
Let's agree to disagree. Let's
earn nine points for GLORY
in Scrabble. You keep score.

TEN THOUSAND HOURS

To compete at the Olympics you must accumulate
ten thousand hours at your sport. When I took piano lessons
from a woman with piano shaped soaps in her bathroom
and piano key embroidered pillows, I gave her three hours
over two years of uncoordinated small handed hammering.
I've invested no time into being statuesque,
nor have I practiced budgeting. If I spent ten thousand hours
on culinary preparation and precision, instead of trying a new recipe
when I tire of beets, I would be certain in my pinch of salt.

LIFT OFF

If every couch available
in your time of need
were stretched end to end
the uneasy tower would reach
the International Space Station,
site of human relationship
experimentation. Close
oxygenless quarters. This month
in space the media describes
complex chemical water filtration
as drinkin' pee. The real test:
open mouth kisses upon touch down.

AMERICA'S NEXT TOP POET

You represent fourteen year olds writers
each line deeply felt down to their accessories.
Every transgendered Aruban with a limp
who has overcome military service,
kitten neglect and a serious rash
is counting on you to represent her dreams.

Your first challenge is to sleep in the home
of a famous dead poet evading security
mimic the ghost's style without mocking.
Hidden cameras will assess your breaking
and entering, poetic posture, line breaks,
and attention to historical hairstyle.

Your panel of anonymous judges
send down their verdict in small
poetry journals proofread by undergraduates
known for their sharp wit and reluctance
toward puns. Your second challenge:
find the journals in their native realm.

In the Ozarks write a sound poem
in the tongue of a native population,
a haiku on the season of your birth
using a cherry blossom dipped
in the liquid representing optimism
but smelling of underachievement.

When you are eliminated, return
to adjunct salary and piles
of student poems. The fan mail
bodily threats and copyright
infringement will pile in your
ANTP brand PO box
unread and unwilling.

PILLOW SONATA

dismantled headphones
plugged to the skeleton
of an aged black plastic P. Jammer
under my pillow
to not disturb your dreams
with the BBC's shrapneled
dictators at a fifth grade level
a strategy that kept Clinton's haircut
populating my dreams all primary long
Hillary drives the school bus
she's a rowdy student in my grocery
on a turbulent ocean fuselage
politi-talk amasses the boundary
my churning insomnia porridge
versus the red velvet armadillo cake
at Robert Mugabe's Bon Voyage
a whole chocolate bowl better
than my own immobilization
job prospects and dirty skillets
avoidance of cold water emotion
aided by mumbling night radio
from my pillow-acute hearing

YOU ARE MIST

Plant your tap root here
        kitchen couch
        yellow cake
        apron string
As good a place
        downpour skirt
        worn out face
        secret life
to tolerate the humidity—
        mossy ticks
        velvet hint
        branch bend swing
There are no hills in history—
        sorghum field
        earthenware
        politics
Most everything slows
        cricket legs
        graduate
        knuckle grove
at this latitude
        cornmeal box
        mockingbird
        Spanish moss
Remember old rules
        candy pants
        shoelaceless
        baseball cleats
Feel your way through
        river rope
        hollow date
        weekends melt

the walls of your choosing
        take a seat
        local stool
        worn out pew
the land of before
        ceiling cracks
        cutting board
        sameness song
This is a call that does not echo
        ominous
        flowers cut
        locket sealed

IN THE AFTERMATH

wall of water drapes your town
wind is named by alphabet
now a 'copter overhead

sea wall, inlet, undertoe
grey demolished house on stilts
no word, wetted memory

one last stretch of earthen berm
gasping plastic tupperware
seals up precious documents

front door, screen porch, off the hinge
soaked consignment precious chair
scared cat, feral underfed

treat with sun your cushioned couch
yellowed walls bleed bleach and sludge
turn what's left to linen rags

THE SOUL WITHIN WOMAN

Her voice deep ash and aged
        throaty backstroke
Years after the wandering uterus
        nailed and stapled
I drew a Canadian map
        guidebook loaned out
To scrape away the windshield's ice
        thumbtack sculpture
This cave unspelunkable
        vocal dreamland
Melodies unmerry indigo plump
        curling tumbler
Exact reminders of large mistakes
        adoption farce
Padded envelope too large for mailbox
        grainy photo
Ample embouchure for hammy carols
        private key brace
I have grown remarkably since
        Myrtle's puppet
Post-polio smoking lessons
        Saskatoon sky
Big-lipped canyon ladies

A MIXTURE OF FRAILTIES

> *—after Susie Mac Murray's sculpture of the same name*

fourteen hundred
washing up gloves

inside out wrong
way round forms a

floor-length gown
rubber smell

enfolds her form
basin placement

mystique signals
running water

eye to spigot
fingertips smooth

protection against
inside churnings

expectations
piercing skin

the dress protects
reaches for you

your dish drainer
mother's teacup

THE MAN BEHIND ME ON THE TRAIN

Noises slip between train headrests
the biological equivalent of queasy-making
chalkboard fingernail gut assault.

Needing much more than a kleenex
entire train car longing for years of lessons
on nuanced clearance of extraneous bodily fluids.

A viscous symphony
only the hyper-perverse would attend
with back-alley tickets and passcode reservations.

He overcomes the difficult acoustics
transportation's cacophony, hairy eyeballs,
and standard daggers of disapproving looks.

Would painfully deformed membranes
or genetic deafness inspire forgiveness
for the trespasses of auditory entrapment?

Certain of parental estrangement,
a mother who never tissued her own.

NIXZMARY

Nixzmary, Nizmary, Nixmarie, your name a lamentation
for an ill-mannered metropolis.
A name we'd praise as evidence of the imaginative.
A name we'd like untethered from its chooser,
the receiver black both eyes
before succumbing to unimaginable inaction—
vapor until its boots meet your noseteeth.
A puzzle in which you must make
new words from the letters "mother."
I cannot fill the space around the chapel with unimaginable.
I look at the pictures of twine and chair chanting
tetherball, tetherball, tetherball to her heartbeat.
Police remove small furniture and the girl
the weight of a four year old.
Every mother.

DE COMPOSE

Questions of the afterlife raised
by the telephone's ring.
People don't like to think about
our consistent march toward filth.
Not an unscrubbed toilet.
Skin cells flaking into dusty corners.
Once you're dead I want to sweep
every remaining tiny compartment
of your organism
to wrap in a microwaved towel
holding your deodorant solid.
Human flesh dissolves faster
than a mouth regenerates taste buds.
I've discovered broccoli lemon
under the yolk of hollandaise.

DISABILITY OF GRIEF

When the answer is awful
and you are thrown a chorus
of howareyous?
Assume the song a ditty
pleading for the pleasant lie.
Sincerity unwelcome
in the cubicled air
where masks are affixed
with extraordinary glues.
Every glimpse of teeth
ghastly reassuring.

AFTER LIFE

Every time we mention the dead
I feel their weight on the mattress
indentations—never flipped.

My pores have forgotten the garlic.

When you die before Americans
learn to love sushi
there is extra unfamiliarity
in the afterlife.

You have to get used to
more than the weight change.

Expecting the rocky coast of Maine
you find Uncle Harry with a beard,
Great Aunt Blanche sitting very still
around an oblong formica table.

There is an abundance of whitefish salad
a surfeit of historically accurate costumes.

Here, this one is exactly your size.

ON THE OCCASION OF EDNA PARKER'S DEATH

With her out of the way
I'm holding the old lady title.
My joints are knotted window screens
wearing almost antebellum sweaters.
At one hundred and fifteen
Guinness is never a beverage,
always a book. You remember
exact price of Indiana bread loaves
and feedlot gossip, but mix
brother's names and flinch when
Jimmy has all his fingers.
You'll need to scoop
the ice cream tonight
I'm the world's oldest woman.

JUVENESCENCE

An architect tells me
the suburbs are pubescent.

Where I learned to smoke,
smooch, insert a tampon.

Street names bolster deceit
Wonderland Dr. and Cinderella Ct.

Spring Creek Parkway
six lanes, no water.

Suburban schooling promises
gun safety, comfortable chairs.

Boundary testers flee to
pull the impalpable taut.

My peers attempt urban
parenting, even if they loved

their progenitors obstinance.
They Zipcar, buy a starter home,

find a place to organize
tools and adult ideas.

BOYS WHO NEED HAIRCUTS

will tell you it's intentional—
not juvenile lion imitation.

Boys who need haircuts
hope to attract girls

who are unselfconscious
about their bra straps.

Unselfconscious girls
are not necessarily

those of adequate
self-esteem. She can

be counted on for categorical
plumage, cautious traipse.

Lockered hallway whispers
a syllable that could be yours.

ADOLESCENCE IS NO JOKE

despite hilarious appearances by Freud
and pus-filled faces. The continuum
of embarrassing moments
could spit you out in an instant
despite your propensity for binge drinking
in an alley or fallow sorghum fields.
The aftermath is the same:
backseat, hotel, hot tub, clinic.
The years between anxiety and
hold-your-own keys, populated
with perpetual reprimands,
clandestine research, full-time
attempts to synthesize the self.

ALPHABET ACROSTIC

After birth criticism demands
every father gives
honest indignation jokingly.
Knuckles Larry manages nuance
often pathetically quotes
rattle snake truths,
underestimates veritable wisdom
x-rays your Z.

ANOTHER ACROSTIC

Calliope love,
My name originates pride,
quells religion, sustains time.
Understand: verseless waters
expound yourself.
Zero around betrothal.
Concentrate down
exquisite fathoms.
Generous? hardly.
I jest.

www.ingramcontent.com/pod-product-compliance
Lightning Source LLC
Chambersburg PA
CBHW022346040426
42449CB00006B/744